MAURICE MAETERLINCK

Pélléas
and Mélisande

TRANSLATED BY

ERVING   WINSLOW

WITH AN INTRODUCTION BY

MONTROSE J. MOSES

Fredonia Books
Amsterdam. The Netherlands

Pélléas and Mélisande

by
Maurice Maeterlinck

ISBN: 1-58963-354-7

In order to make original editions of historical works
available to scholars at an economical price, this
facsimile of the original edition of 1894 is
reproduced from the best available copy and has
been digitally enhanced to improve legibility, but the
text remains unaltered to retain historical
authenticity.

To

OCTAVE MIRBEAU

AS A TESTIMONY OF DEEP FRIENDSHIP

ADMIRATION, AND GRATITUDE

M. M.

INTRODUCTION

To understand Maurice Maeterlinck aright, you must realize the fabric from which he has built his philosophy — his fragments of philosophy, it were best to say, since they can not as yet be reduced to a system. Unseeable protagonists are most potent in his dramas; the presence of Death is almost always lurking near; Life, with exterior and interior manifestations, is an active flow of forces, realizable only from within; and Fate, shorn of its formal religious meaning, is the central pivot of all growth and of all development. The fact is, as M. Soissons asserts, that "modern mysticism in art has lost its former note of religious asceticism, its unearthly character, and has rather become scientific."

In *Pélléas et Mélisande* we are made to experience a brooding sense. "Unless we close our eyes we are always deceived," exclaims Arkel, the epitome of wisdom, the example of Browning's "the last of life for which the first was made." "Never do useless events occur," he adds. And Mélisande, fearing, trembles over something stronger than herself. Necessity becomes one of the elements that help to form life and to shape destiny. In that castle of dark sunshine, tangibleness of feeling is lost in the strange terrifying of presentiment. Here the sage is given to weigh the justice of events; in the midst of lifting gloom there always lurks the shadow of unlooked-for consequences.

The light of day appears to frighten souls; does not Mélisande whisper to Pélléas : " I feel nearer to you in the dark " ? Unrelenting seems that Fate which makes Death stalk ever nigh the young, in preference to the old. Pélléas believes that "those who love are always sad." In this world where there is so much we shall never know, there are many, like Mélisande, who are born, as the Doctor says, " by chance to die," and in the end

" she dies by chance." In this atmosphere of hesitant utterance faintly limned figures grope for words to give expression to their weeping souls. Maeterlinck, in his dramas, is disciple of the unexpressed ; to him, as to Goethe and Carlyle, silence is golden.

All this spectral background to Maeterlinck's theatre later became the framework for his prose philosophy. *The Treasure of the Humble, Wisdom and Destiny, The Life of the Bee, The Buried Temple, The Double Garden,* — each one of them deals with the mystery of becoming, of being; in common they analyze Luck and Chance and Justice ; not satisfied with the mere appearance of beauty, they search inwardly for the essence.

Pélléas et Mélisande is part of a dramatic theory which was practised before it was preached; it involved a scene, saturated with the vapor of something always impending; the flesh melted into the essence of the presence felt, rather than of the presence seen. We find in this theatre of Maeterlinck a new wording, a new color, a new feeling, a new totality of effect; we handle no longer substance, but the shadow. Maeterlinck and Ibsen stand at equal distances from Life, but at opposite poles: Ibsen with the scalpel, cutting in toward Truth as he sees it; Maeterlinck working toward Life from the essence of the abstract.

While Maeterlinck is at the same time a mystic, a symbolist, and a transcendentalist in his philosophy, he is still more a poet who is noticeably affected by the scientific truths of his age. It is science, as Soissons again avers, which has destroyed the deceptions of mediæval mysticism, which has forced a recognition of the *two* sides of the essence of things — the ideal factor and the real factor. Maeterlinck's study of the bee is an exquisite example of the fine balance of these two conditions.

He deals with soul pigments as an artist deals with colors; he makes use of the external world only in so far as it is necessary to produce spiritual effects. And because of his dependence upon extraordinary detail, we might well criticise him for

MAURICE MAETERLINCK.
Author of " Pélléas and Mélisande."

the mechanism which plays so important a part in his little dramas — storms, starlight, the whistle of the wind — were it not for the artful way in which he places spiritual values upon the very machinery or accessory itself; for example, the passages with Pélléas and Mélisande in the cave of the fathomless pools, or the essay on the automobile, which might well be contrasted in literary treatment of externals with Kipling's *The Ship That Found Herself.* As regards the nature scenery in this spectral theatre, the paths are sketched by a light which penetrates from an exterior brilliancy, and the consequence is that more massiveness is added to the gloom within.

It is with the philosophy of Maeterlinck's style that we have to deal, rather than with his philosophy of life — the one almost includes the other. *Pélléas et Mélisande* stands fifth in his dramatic progression; * it forms one of his three direct

---

* Thus far the Maeterlinckean theatre comprises: *La Princesse Maleine* (1889), *L'Intruse, Les Aveugles* (1890), *Les Sept Princesses* (1891), *Pélléas et Mélisande* (1892), *Alladine et Palomides, Intérieur, La Mort de Tintagiles*

reversions to material already used by others ; or, rather, we should say, there are three plays which mark in him literary influences. In his first drama, *La Princesse Maleine* (1889), he was extravagantly greeted by M. Octave Mirbeau (to whom *Pélléas et Mélisande* is dedicated) as the " Belgian Shakespeare " and like all over-enthusiastic friends, this critic drew down upon the youthful poet the prejudice which comes when a hasty comparison is made with *Hamlet*.

In the working out of his shadowy suggestions, Maeterlinck has undoubtedly read

---

— *trois petits drames pour Marionnettes* (1894), *Aglavaine et Sélysette* (1896), *Ariane et Barbe-Bleue, Sœur Béatrice* (1901), *Monna Vanna* (1902), and *Joyzelle* (1903).

Maeterlinck is also the author of the following minor works, which none the less are important in his intellectual development: *Serres Chaudes* (1889; small volume of verse in obscure and undeveloped form), *L'Ornement des Noces Spirituelles* (translation from the Flemish of Jean Ruysbroeck, with an introduction, 1891), *Les Disciples à Sais et les Fragments de Novalis* (translation from the German, with an introduction, 1895), a tragedy by John Ford, under title of *Annabella*, for Théâtre de l'Œuvre (this translation is not included in his collected works).

M Maeterlinck also wrote an introduction for Mlle. Mali's translation of a few of Emerson's Essays. Brussels: Paul La Comblez.

his poets. It is no sin to claim inspiration from Shakespeare, or to acknowledge indebtedness to Browning's *Luria* for suggestions in *Monna Vanna*, or to draw material from the *Miracles of Notre-Dame* for the story of *Sister Beatrice*, or to turn once more to the most dominant symbolist of all poets, Dante, for his Francesca episode. Neither is it hopeless to acknowledge by the very gloom of his atmosphere that Poe — through the medium, no doubt, of Verlaine's sympathetic translations, — gave an impetus to his technique, which he now appears to have partly outgrown. The difference, however, between Maeterlinck and Poe is that while the former could easily slip from any shadow of the latter's influence, Poe never could escape the shadow of himself.

If Mr. Richard Hovey was right in claiming that Maeterlinck has, like Baudelaire, created a new shudder, we might add that the shudder is not a constitutional weakness. In fact it seems to me that here lies a point of grievance against M. Maeterlinck, the dramatist. Seeking particular spiritual effects, he is virtually responsible as an artist for the means by which those effects are gained. Has it not been proved that the imminent presence may just as readily be felt in the ebullition of joy, like that experienced in Wordsworth's *Skylark*, as in the dark murkiness of dank caves ? Such deep gloom as Maeterlinck has persisted in using has always accompanied certain romantic tendencies.

Maeterlinck's dialogue is unlike that of any other living dramatist or poet; its chief sign of recognition lies in the repetition of broken sentences — a repetition, a parallelism which, from a psycho-physical basis, is the lyrical outcome of peculiar nervous pressure. In ordinary reading such fragmentary speech appears unnecessarily simple; it is often spoken of derisively as the Ollendorf nursery talk, and at one time challenged the wrath of Max Nordau.

There are those who are prone to discount Maeterlinck's own critical exposé of his theatre; who class his remarks with Poe's self-analysis of *The Raven* in the remarkably clever essay on *The Philosophy of Composition* ; but Poe's method was a bravado attitude, while Maeterlinck's was not.

In his paper *On the Tragedies of Shakespeare, Considered with Reference to Their Fitness for Stage Representation*, Charles Lamb asserted that the meditation of Hamlet or of Othello was not suited to become the object of external interest and curiosity. Here is a point which Maeterlinck contends and he refers to Elia as one of his chief supporters. Moreover, it is generally conceded that Charles van Lerberghe, when he wrote his dramatic episode, *Les Flaireurs*, furnished his Belgian contemporary with a form and a manner of dealing with destiny which dominate such psychological sketches as *The Intruder* and *The Blind*. The real stage of both is not external, but lies within the imagination.

When Maeterlinck had penned these " infantile " dramas he was firm in his belief that one person, alone in a room with the invisible forces of life surging around

him, and, unconscious of all laws, whether
of silence or of sound, of light or of darkness, submissively awaiting his destiny —
that such a figure was living a fuller life
than the flamboyant general or the lover
at the maximum pitch of his passion.

Such is the background for Maeterlinck's
dramatic theory; he confesses this in his
preface to an early edition of his plays.
He asserts : I do not write for ordinary
actors; I believe that poems die the moment they are outwardly expressed. The
Macbeth and the Hamlet that we see are
not the Macbeth and the Hamlet of the
book; a thought which is meant for the
soul takes flight at the spoken word. Something of Hamlet dies as soon as we see him
dying on the stage.

Thus this negative playwright becomes
more negative when he declares that "the
theatre is a place where masterpieces die;
for the production of a masterpiece by
means of accidental and human elements
has something *antinomic* in itself." He
approaches his static theatre with the state-
ment that every masterpiece is a symbol,

CLAUDE DEBUSSY.
Composer of the Opera " Pélléas and Mélisande."

and a symbol cannot bear the active presence of a man. Did not the Greeks, he further argues, recognize the essential demand of the spirit by using the mask; was not the Elizabethan declamation *melopœian?*

However, the advance of Maurice Maeterlinck is to be found in his future denial that the best and truest in life or in drama lies in the unexplainable. From the gasping iteration of dialogue in *The Princess Maleine* he has passed into the full rounded utterances of *Monna Vanna*; from the mere suggestion of spiritual states to situations that visibly change. Profundity no longer has the meaning of quiescence ; drama slips from the *static* into the *dynamic*.

In one of his latest utterances, an essay on the *Modern Drama,* included in *The Double Garden,* Maeterlinck accentuates his belief that external action in drama is to-day considered secondary to deeper motive ; that besides penetrating into spiritual states, audiences and readers are also demanding a new beauty " that shall be less abstract than was the old." On

the strength of this attitude Mr. William
Archer declares that M. Maeterlinck has
reached the mental and spiritual position
of Ibsen's Emperor Julian, where "the old
beauty is no longer beautiful, and the new
truth is not yet true." He will now, in
his dramatic apostasy, so far yield as to
draw his interior view nearer to the practical necessities of the theatrical scene.
Somehow, Maeterlinck is striving for that
third empire where the spirit and dramatic
expression may become reconciled; may,
in fact, be made one. He has so far come
nearest success in this idea throughout the
situations in *Monna Vanna*. The creeping
paralysis of external action in the modern
play, which he so sincerely welcomes, has
possibly narrowed the romantic, the heroic,
the picturesque setting, but in his own
work Maeterlinck no longer questions the
necessity for a tangible background.

Take the striking dramatic sketch, en-
titled *Home (Intérieur)*, the whole tragedy
of which occurs in a room where silent
figures move, while, outside, the dialogue
of those bringing death into the uncon-

scious group breathes forth that atmosphere of impending Fate which can only be
produced through the consummate art
of Maeterlinck's technique. Speech in the
garden is more than interpolative of the
situation as seen through the window, —
in fact, the garden is of no material value
as measured with the spiritual intensity of
the scene suggested; the imagination is
stimulated to that point where a mere
outline carries one the remainder of the
way. The ether is breathless, ominous.

Examine *The Intruder* — Death, coming
through an atmospheric medium created
by the conscious nervousness of three
people subject to super-sensitive expect-
ancy. Contrast this with the appearance
of Death in *Everyman,* and you will
measure the difference between a moral
allegory and a subtle mood. The appearance of the ghost of Hamlet's
father is crudely handled beside the skill
of Maeterlinck's impressionistic touch.
His stage directions breathe forth oppres-
siveness; the elements stir restlessly; the
qualities of different souls are distinguish-

able by the manner in which these souls respond to the pregnant silence; they almost rustle like the fine texture of silk. Fear, dread, suspicion, undue noises, and finally a Sister of Charity announcing the ravishes of death, and pointing beyond the door to where the dead body lies — this is the close tragedy of a single room, the oppressive world which Maeterlinck creates by filmy suggestion.

The Blind is still more symbolic — but there is something physical beneath the allegory, an allegory which suggests that in the midst of the unseeing world, of blind humanity, the Church might stand as dead with no one to recognize the fact. But there is also the unerring picture of the psychological and physiological state of the actual blind; it is not merely a spiritual groping which Maeterlinck suggests, but a local inability, and the unusual strain upon a nervous system consequent therefrom. Here is the suggestion of Poe at his greatest height. One needs must smile over the directions as to scenery; how shall we ever be able to depict

a Norland forest " with an eternal look " !
Yet the surroundings are gruesome enough,
and nature with her weeping willows
seems to blossom in accordance with mental states. Poe could not have been more
utterly destitute of hope, of potential
brightness. Had Maeterlinck been seeking to outrival *The Fall of the House of
Usher ?*

All of these elements are to be traced in
Pélléas et Mélisande. Turn to the significant visit of Golaud and Pélléas to the
stagnant vaults of the castle in Act III.;
do you not catch the sepulchral odor
of *The Blind ?* Re-read *The Death of
Tintagiles,* and compare it with the opening of the third act, or with the pastoral
sketch of Yniold and the Shepherd;
Maeterlinck's children are older in their
tender ignorance than his heroines with
their half-knowledge which only mystifies.
Yet these heroines are all related; they
are of the same quality in *La Princesse
Maleine,* in *Aglavaine et Sélysette,* and in
Pélléas et Mélisande. And strange to say,
though created at different times, these

yielding characters were all born, to judge by their spiritual relationship, at the same moment within the mind of the dramatist.

There have been two great obstacles in Maeterlinck's path leading to the theatre. He has been viewed with a dazed understanding, because of the misuse of the term "mystic," and again he has been unduly identified with his early dramatic formulas. These latter have become modified, but have not yet counteracted the old impression.

The mystic, as one whose efforts are directed toward a full realization of the inner life, should not be confounded with the obscurist. Mr. Arthur Symons very accurately differentiates the infinite from the indefinite, and insists that "a mystic hates the vague with a more profound hatred than any other artist." Indeed, I cannot recognize the obscurity in Maeterlinck as an essayist which he is popularly supposed to exhibit. He has come from darkness into light; he has carried his dramas from an almost impossible vagueness to stability of form and motive; he

MISS MARY GARDEN.
Creator of the rôle of " Mélisande " in both France and America.

has applied his philosophy to human problems, and is no longer content to regard existence in the abstract.

Where in his puppet plays he has heretofore dealt insistently with Death, Maeterlinck's essays seem to show him now more and more solicitous concerning the facts of Life. He is a poet philosophizing upon every-day existence acted upon by uncommon forces; he draws inspiration from the mystics, but his spirit is not aloof; he strives to touch earth, to bring his hypotheses, as he says, to accord with the experiences of every-day struggles. Emerson did not care particularly whether or not he obtained any practical results; he brought home to plain, honest, thoroughgoing citizens the realization of their God-like qualities, but, like Matthew Arnold, he did not suggest the lowly means, the earthly means, by which those qualities might be developed. Yet Emerson was more of the citizen himself than Maeterlinck, despite his isolation at Concord, and though he influenced Maeterlinck, he was not as closely in touch with him as was Marcus Aurelius. Somewhere Maeterlinck has expressed the difference and the reason by claiming for the latter a position more nearly akin to pure thought, while Emerson was a sage of commonplace days, apparelling the man in the street with celestial light.

Those who heard the opening performance of Debussy's music-drama of *Pélléas et Mélisande* at the Manhattan Opera House went away doubting whether they really understood the orchestration. Had Mr. Hammerstein softened the lights on the stage to a semi-darkness or swung a gauze curtain across the front of the scene as Mrs. Patrick Campbell did in her production of the play; had Miss Mary Garden, despite the fresh spirit of her acting, been less substantial in her movements, these same folk would have read still more into this pale tragedy of child-like love. There is no more symbolism in *Pélléas et Mélisande* than there is in every work of art that has beauty for its theme. Once let it be whispered that a poet is a mystic — as though we were not all mystics ! — and there will be read into him what is not there at all.

When Claude Debussy wrote his score for *Pélléas et Mélisande* (1893–1895), his aim was to produce in sound as shadowy an atmosphere as Maeterlinck had given to his marionette theatre. Already Debussy had allied himself with the mystics by his songs to the words of Rossetti, Verlaine, and Mallarmé. But on the first production of his larger work in Paris, at the Opéra-Comique, on April 30, 1902, a storm of critical opinion followed and had by no means subsided when Mr. Oscar Hammerstein, with commendable artistic daring, assembled the same cast of principals at his Manhattan Opera House (New York), and made the evening of February 19, 1908, a distinctive date by giving *Pélléas et Mélisande* its American premiere. Yet, despite the beauty of the woodland scenes, despite the expressive acting and phrasing of Miss Garden, M. Périer and M. Dufrane, — despite the occasional liquid run of harps, as when Mélisande's wedding-ring splashes into the

Fountain of the Blind, — the music undoubtedly stung and blistered and pained
and outraged the ear, if we may use Mr.
Henry Krehbiel's estimate. The score is
thoroughly unmelodic; the voices are con-
fined to the limits of the Gregorian chant;
the love passages have none of the seduc-
tiveness of *Tristan and Isolde;* the nature
motives suggest none of the mystery or
freshness of *Siegfried,* none of the dream
quality of Hauptmann's *The Sunken Bell.*
In fact, there are passages that drag; the
last act, where Mélisande's death should
have been the signal for the gathering
together of all the preceding motives, is
unnecessarily monotone, though Miss
Garden's lyric simplicity added much to
the scene. Debussy's thematic handling
confuses, and because he does not believe in
the *chanson,* he sacrifices some significant
scenes that would have been treated effec-
tively by a musician of the "Carmen"
school.

This much, however, may be said of the
music of *Pélléas et Mélisande* — apart from
the technical consideration of its chord

resolutions: despite the absence of lin-
gering arias, the beauties of its orchestration become more pronounced after repeated hearing. Debussy's desire seems
to have been to show that the emotion of
character and the emotion produced by the
music itself are not separately felt, but
are mingled simultaneously. He attempts
to effect this commingling by dispensing
with all formal musical phrases. He has
claimed that he is more of a reformer than
Wagner, since he places no value upon the
past in musical development. On the face
of it this is sweeping, since he has so per-
sistently thrown himself upon the re-
sources of the Gregorian chant.

As Maeterlinck has overridden convention in drama, so has Debussy overridden
convention in music. He will doubtless
modify or develop his theory as Maeterlinck has modified and developed his. I
am tempted to predict that in the years to
come the score for *Pélléas et Mélisande*
will take its place with the countless
operas of *Francesca da Rimini* now forgotten. For what, after all, is this drama

of Maeterlinck's but the Dante episode in another form?

Maeterlinck suggests music; this may be because his marionette plays are moods, and are, in themselves, mental states which in turn attempt to create mental states; they are better fitted to a wordless medium. And evidently Debussy tried his utmost to create for himself a musical theory which would, by means of incongruous harmonies, make his musical symbol two-fold — sound and super-sound.

Yet, after we have struggled through the vague in orchestration and in dialogue, we return to the ultimate conclusion. All that Maeterlinck requires in his dramas is for us to recognize that there is an intimate beauty, an interior value, an essence, more real and more true than the object which symbolizes it.

MONTROSE J. MOSES.

PÉLLÉAS AND MÉLISANDE

PÉLLÉAS AND MÉLISANDE.

CHARACTERS.

Arkël, king of Allemonde.

Geneviève, mother of Pélléas and Golaud.

Pélléas,
Golaud, } grandsons of Arkél.

Mélisande.

Little Yniold, son of Golaud and a deceased wife

A physician.

The porter.

Servants, beggars, etc.

ACT I.

SCENE I.

THE ENTRANCE TO THE CASTLE.

SERVANTS (*within*).
Open the door !   Open the door !

THE PORTER (*within*).
Who is there ?   Why do you wake me ?
Use the side doors — use the side doors ;
there are enough of them !...

A MAID–SERVANT (*within*).
We have to wash the sill, the door, and
the steps.   Open it for us !   Open it !

ANOTHER MAID–SERVANT (*within*).
There are to be wonderful doings !

THIRD MAID–SERVANT (*within*).
There is to be a great festival.   Quick,
open the door !...

THE SERVANTS (*within*).
Oh, open it, open it !

THE PORTER (*within*).
Be patient ! Be patient ! I know not
whether I can open it... It is so seldom
used... Wait till daylight !...

FIRST MAID-SERVANT (*within*).
It is light enough outside. I see the
sun through the chinks...

THE PORTER (*within*).
Here are the great keys !... Oh ! how
the locks and bolts grate !... Help me start
them...

THE MAID-SERVANTS (*within*).
We are pulling, we are pulling now...

SECOND MAID-SERVANT (*within*).
It will not open...

FIRST MAID-SERVANT (*within*).
Ah ! it is beginning to move ! It moves
a little !

THE PORTER (*within*).
How it creaks, how it creaks ! It will
awaken every one !...

"WHENCE DID YOU COME?"

SECOND MAID–SERVANT (*appearing on threshold*).

Oh! how light it is already out of doors.

FIRST MAID–SERVANT.

The sun is rising over the sea.

THE PORTER.

At last it is open... It is wide open!

(*All the maid-servants appear and come out hastily*).

FIRST MAID–SERVANT.

I am going to clean the sill at once...

SECOND MAID–SERVANT.

We can never get this all clean.

OTHER MAID–SERVANTS.

Bring water! Bring water!

THE PORTER.

Yes, yes; pour the water over it, pour the water over it! If you should pour all the water of the Deluge you would never accomplish your task...

SCENE II.

A FOREST.

(Mélisande is discovered by a spring. Golaud enters.)

GOLAUD.

I cannot find my way out of this forest. — Heaven knows where that beast has led me. And yet I believe I must have done for it — here are the marks of its blood. But now I have lost it and it seems I have lost myself too, and the dogs have gone off on a false scent. I must try to retrace my steps — I hear some one weeping...

Ha! what is that by the spring? — A young girl weeping by the spring! *(He coughs.)* She hears me not. I cannot see her face. *(He approaches and touches Mélisande's shoulder.)* Why do you weep? *(Mélisande trembles, draws herself up, and is about to run away.)* Be not afraid! There is nothing to fear. Why are you weeping here all by yourself?

MÉLISANDE.

Do not touch me, do not touch me!

GOLAUD.

Do not fear... I will not... oh, how beautiful you are!

MÉLISANDE.

Do not touch me! Do not touch me, or I will jump into the water!...

GOLAUD.

I will not touch you, then... See, I will stay by this tree. Do not fear! Has any one harmed you?

MÉLISANDE.

Oh! yes, yes, yes!...

(She sobs bitterly.)

GOLAUD.

Who has harmed you?

MÉLISANDE.

Every one! every one!

GOLAUD.

How have you been harmed?

MÉLISANDE.

I will not tell. I cannot tell!...

GOLAUD.

Come, come, you must not weep so. Whence did you come?

MÉLISANDE.

Oh, I ran away... I ran away... ran away !...

GOLAUD.

But where did you come from ?

MÉLISANDE.

I am lost !... lost !... Oh, I am lost in this place... I do not belong here !... This is not my native place.

GOLAUD.

What is your native place ? What is your native place ?

MÉLISANDE.

Oh, far away,... far, very far from here.

GOLAUD.

What is that shining thing down in the water ?

MÉLISANDE.

Where ? — Ah, that is the crown he gave me ! — It fell while I was weeping...

GOLAUD.

A crown ? — Who gave you a crown ? — I will try to get it for you...

MÉLISANDE.

No, no. I do not want it again! I do
not want it... I had rather die... die at
once...

GOLAUD.

I could easily reach it. The water is
not very deep.

MÉLISANDE.

I do not want it again. If you get it I
will throw myself in !...

GOLAUD.

No, no. I will let it stay — though it
could be easily reached. It seems very
beautiful. — Is it long since you fled ?

MÉLISANDE.

Oh, yes... Who are you ?

GOLAUD.

I am Prince Golaud, the grandson of
Arkël, the old King of Allemonde...

MÉLISANDE.

But your hair is already gray...

GOLAUD.

Yes ; a little, here on the temples...

MÉLISANDE.

Your beard is gray, too... Why do you look at me so ?

GOLAUD.

I am looking at your eyes. — Do you never close them ?

MÉLISANDE.

Yes, yes ; I shut them at night...

GOLAUD.

Why do you look so startled ?

MÉLISANDE.

Are you a giant ?

GOLAUD.

I am a man like other men...

MÉLISANDE.

How happened you to come this way ?

GOLAUD.

I am sure I do not know. I was hunting in the forest. I was on the track of a boar. I lost my way. — You look like a mere child. How old are you ?

MÉLISANDE.

I am growing cold...

GOLAUD.

Will you come with me?

MÉLISANDE.

No, no. I will stay here...

GOLAUD.

You cannot stay here alone. You cannot be here all night by yourself... What is your name?

MÉLISANDE.

Mélisande.

GOLAUD.

You cannot stay here, Mélisande. Come with me...

MÉLISANDE.

I shall stay here...

GOLAUD.

You will be afraid all by yourself. No one knows what might happen to you here... all night... alone. It is impossible. Mélisande, come, give me your hand...

MÉLISANDE.

Oh, do not touch me!...

GOLAUD.

Do not scream... I will not touch you again. But come with me. The night

will be very dark and very cold.   Come
with me...

MÉLISANDE.

Whither ?...

GOLAUD.

I do not know...   I too am lost...

(*They go out.*)

SCENE III.

A HALL IN THE CASTLE.

(*Arkël and Geneviève are discovered.*)

GENEVIÈVE.

This is his letter to his brother Pélléas :
" I found her weeping, one evening, by
a spring when I was lost in the forest.   I
know neither her age, nor whence she comes,
nor who she is, and I dare not question
her.   She must have had some awful
fright, for if she is asked to tell about the
past she only answers like a child with
passionate tears, which are terrible to see.
When I found her near the spring, a
crown of gold had just dropped from her
head and fallen into the water.   She was

dressed like a princess, though her clothes
were all torn by the briers. It is six
months now since we were married, and I
am as ignorant of her past as the day we
met. Meanwhile, dear Pélléas, whom I
love more than a brother although we
were not begotten by the same father,
prepare them to receive us... I know my
mother will gladly forgive me. But I
dread the king, I dread Arkël my grandfather, notwithstanding all his goodness,
for I have deranged all his political ar-
rangements by my marriage, and I tremble
lest even Mélisande's beauty should not
excuse what his wisdom may count as a
folly. If, however, he will consent to receive her as he would receive a daughter of his own, light a lamp upon the
summit of the tower overlooking the
sea, the third night after you receive this
letter. I shall be able to see it from our
vessel. If I see no light, I shall pass on
and return no more."... What have you to
say?

ARKËL.

Nothing. He has probably done for the

best. I am a very old man, and yet I have
never been able to understand myself; how
then can I judge others? I am not far
from the grave, and I do not even know
how to judge my own actions... Unless
we close our eyes we are always deceived.
This may seem strange to us — but that is
all. He is already past middle life, and
like an impulsive boy he has married a
young girl whom he found by a spring. It
may seem strange to us because we see
only the wrong side of others' fates —
even the wrong side of our own... Until
this happened he has alway been guided
by my counsel. I thought the hand of
the Princess Ursula, which I wanted to
secure for him, would make him happy... He
could not live alone, and since his wife's
death he has been forlorn, and then that
alliance would have terminated long wars
and old animosities... He has not acceded
to my wish. Let it be as he has chosen. I
have never striven to counteract another's
fate. He knows better than I what he de-
sires to make of his future life. Never,
perhaps, do useless events occur...

GENEVIÈVE.

He has always been so wise, so grave and strong !... I could have understood it in Pélléas... But he— at his age ! Who is this girl he is bringing to us ? — A stranger found in the wood !... Since his wife died, he seemed to live only for his son, little Yniold, and if he ever thought of marrying again, it was only because you desired it... And now !... A child out of the forest !... He has forgotten all the past !... What shall we do ?...

(Enter Pélléas.)

ARKËL.

Who is that ?

GENEVIÈVE.

It is Pélléas ? He has been weeping.

ARKËL.

Is it you, Pélléas ? — Come a little nearer that I may be able to see you — here where it is lighter...

PÉLLÉAS.

Grandfather, I received at the same time with my brother's letter another letter — a letter from my friend Marcellus... He

is dying, and he asks me to come to him
before he dies...

ARKËL.

Must you   go before your   brother
comes? — Perhaps your friend is not so
ill as he thinks...

PÉLLÉAS.

His letter is so sad that I can read death
between the lines...   He predicts the very
day that he shall die...   He tells me I have
time, if I hasten, to get to him, but there
is none to lose.   It is a very long journey,
and if I wait for Golaud's return it may
be too late...

ARKËL.

But you must wait a little while...   We
know not what your brother's return may
bring forth.   Besides, is not your father
here in the room above worse perhaps than
your friend ?...   Can you hesitate between
father and friend ?...

(*He goes out.*)

GENEVIÈVE.

Be sure the lamp is lit from this evening
on, Pélléas.

(*They go out at opposite doors.*)

SCENE IV.

EXTERIOR OF THE CASTLE.

(*Enter Geneviève and Mélisande.*)

MÉLISANDE.

It is dark in the garden. And what forests, what forests all about the palace !...

GENEVIÈVE.

Yes ; that struck me with surprise when I first came here, as it does every one. There are parts of the wood where the sun's light hardly penetrates even at noon. But one soon grows accustomed to the gloom... It is long, long ago — forty years since I came... Look the other way, you can see the shining of the sea...

MÉLISANDE.

I hear a sound below...

GENEVIÈVE.

Yes, some one is coming up... Ah, it is Pélléas... He seems still weary from having waited so long for your arrival...

MÉLISANDE.

He does not see us.

GENEVIÈVE.

I think he saw us, but he is undecided
what to do... Pélléas, Pélléas, is it you ?

PÉLLÉAS.

Yes !... I have been down to the sea...

GENEVIÈVE.

And so have we. We wanted to find
some light. There it is lighter than else-
where ; and yet the sea is gloomy.

PÉLLÉAS.

We shall have a storm to-night. There
has been one every night for some time,
and yet it is so calm now... It would be
easy to put to sea in such weather, yet we
should never see land again.

MÉLISANDE.

There is something leaving the port
now...

PÉLLÉAS.

It must be a great ship... The lights are
very high on its mast head ; we can see it...
soon, when it passes that opening...

GENEVIÈVE.

I think we shall not be able to see it...
There is a fog on the sea...

"IT IS THE SHIP IN WHICH I CAME!"

PÉLLÉAS.
The fog seems to be lifting slowly...

MÉLISANDE.
Yes, I see down there a little light which was not there before.

PÉLLÉAS.
That is a lighthouse. There are several others which we cannot see as yet.

MÉLISANDE.
The ship is in the opening... It is already far away...

PÉLLÉAS.
It is a foreign vessel. It seems to me larger than any of ours...

MÉLISANDE.
It is the ship in which I came!...

PÉLLÉAS.
She has all sail spread now...

MÉLISANDE.
It is the ship in which I came. She has such great sails... I know her by her sails...

PÉLLÉAS.
There will be a storm to-night...

MÉLISANDE.

Why does she sail to-night ?... She has
nearly disappeared... And she may be
wrecked !...

PÉLLÉAS.

How quickly it is growing dark !...

(Silence.)

GENEVIÈVE.

Why does no one speak ?... Have neither
of you anything to say ?... It is time to go
in. Pélléas, take Mélisande, she does not
know the way. I must go to look for little
Yniold.

(She goes out.)

PÉLLÉAS.

There is nothing to be seen now on the
sea...

MÉLISANDE.

I see more lights.

PÉLLÉAS.

Those are the other lighthouses... Do
you hear the sea ?... The wind is rising.
Let us go down this way. Give me your
hand.

MÉLISANDE.

Look, look; my hands are full...

PÉLLÉAS.

I will take your arm, the path is steep and it is very dark... I may be going away to-morrow...

MÉLISANDE.

Oh !... why are you going ?

(*They go out.*)

ACT II.

SCENE I.

A FOUNTAIN IN THE PARK.

(Enter Pélléas and Mélisande.)

PÉLLÉAS.

You do not know this place to which
I have brought you? — I often come here
at noontime when it is too warm in the
garden. It is stifling to-day even under
the shadow of the trees.

MÉLISANDE.

Oh, how clear the water is!...

PÉLLÉAS.

It is as cool as ice. This is an old
abandoned fountain! The story runs that
it was once a miraculous fountain. It
opened the eyes of the blind. — It is still
called "The Fountain of the Blind."

"THIS IS AN OLD ABANDONED FOUNTAIN."

MÉLISANDE.

Will it no longer open the eyes of the blind ?

PÉLLÉAS.

Since the king himself is almost blind, people have lost faith in it...

MÉLISANDE.

What a lonely place !... How quiet it is !

PÉLLÉAS.

It is always strangely quiet here !... Even the water seems asleep... Will you sit down on this marble coping of the basin ? The linden yonder keeps the sun away...

MÉLISANDE.

I will lie on the marble slab. — I want to look down to the bottom of the water...

PÉLLÉAS.

It cannot be seen. — It is as deep as the sea itself. — No one knows whence it comes. — Perhaps it comes from the very bowels of the earth...

MÉLISANDE.

If anything bright were at the bottom, it would perhaps be seen...

PÉLLÉAS.

Do not lean so far over !...

MÉLISANDE.

I want to touch the water...

PÉLLÉAS.

Take care you do not lose your balance...
Let me hold you by the hand...

MÉLISANDE.

No, no; I want to put both my hands
deep down into the water... They are so
feverish to-day...

PÉLLÉAS.

Oh, take care, take care...   Mélisande !...
Mélisande !... — Oh, your hair !

MÉLISANDE *(drawing back)*.

I cannot, I cannot reach it !...

PÉLLÉAS.

Your hair was falling into the water...

MÉLISANDE.

Yes, my hair is longer than my arms !...
It is longer than I am !...

(Silence.)

PÉLLÉAS.

Was it not by a fountain also that he found you?

MÉLISANDE.

Yes...

PÉLLÉAS.

What did he say to you?

MÉLISANDE.

Nothing... I do not remember...

PÉLLÉAS.

Did he come close to you?

MÉLISANDE.

Yes — he tried to kiss me...

PÉLLÉAS.

And you did not allow it?

MÉLISANDE.

No.

PÉLLÉAS.

Why did you not allow it?

MÉLISANDE.

Oh, oh, I just saw something moving at the bottom !...

PÉLLÉAS.

Take care, take care ! — you will fall in ! — What have you playing with there?

MÉLISANDE.

The ring he gave me.

PÉLLÉAS.

Take care, you will lose it...

MÉLISANDE.

No, no, my hands are steady...

PÉLLÉAS.

Do not play with it, where the water is so deep...

MÉLISANDE.

My hold is secure.

PÉLLÉAS.

How it shines in the sun! — Do not throw it up so to the sky...

MÉLISANDE.

Ah!...

PÉLLÉAS.

Did it fall ?

MÉLISANDE.

It fell into the water !...

PÉLLÉAS.

Where is it, where is it ?...

MÉLISANDE.

I do not see it sink...

PÉLLÉAS.
I think I see it glitter...

MÉLISANDE.
My ring ?

PÉLLÉAS.
Yes, yes ; see there !...

MÉLISANDE.
Oh, it is too deep — no, no ; that is not it !... That is not it !... It is lost, lost — there is only a circle on the water... what can we do ?... What are we to do now ?...

PÉLLÉAS.
It is no use to fret so about a ring. It is nothing... I dare say it can be recovered, or we can get another just like it...

MÉLISANDE.
No, no ; we shall never find it, we shall never get another... I thought I had caught it safe in my hand... I had already shut my hand, and nevertheless it fell in spite of me... I threw it too high, toward the sun !...

PÉLLÉAS.
Come, come, we will return some other time... Come, it is time. They will be com-

ing to look for us.   It was striking twelve
just as the ring fell.

MÉLISANDE.

What shall we say if Golaud asks where
it is ?

PÉLLÉAS.

The truth, the truth, the truth !...

(They go out.)

SCENE II.

AN APARTMENT IN THE CASTLE.

(*Golaud is discovered lying on a bed.
Mélisande is by his side.*)

GOLAUD.

Ah! ah! everything is going well.   It
will amount to nothing.   I cannot understand how it happened.   I was hunting
quietly in the forest.   My horse swerved
suddenly with no apparent cause.   Could he
have seen something ?...   It was just after
the stroke of noon.   At the twelfth rever-
beration he suddenly grew wild and dashed
blindly and madly against a tree.   That

was the last I saw and heard. I remember nothing more. I fell and he must have fallen on me. When I recovered consciousness it seemed as though the whole forest was on my chest; my very heart seemed crushed. But my heart is sound. It seems there was no real harm done...

MÉLISANDE.

Will you drink a little water?

GOLAUD.

No, no, thank you, I am not thirsty.

MÉLISANDE.

Will you have another pillow?... There is a little spot of blood on this.

GOLAUD.

No, no, it is not worth while. I had a bleeding from the mouth just now. It may return.

MÉLISANDE.

Are you sure?... You are not suffering?

GOLAUD.

No, no, I have had many others like this. I am made of iron and blood...

These are not children's bones. Do not
worry about me...

MÉLISANDE.

Close your eyes and try to sleep... I
shall stay here to-night.

GOLAUD.

No, no, I cannot have you tire yourself
thus. I need nothing. I shall sleep like
a child... What is the matter, Mélisande?
What makes you weep all of a sudden?...

MÉLISANDE *(sobbing)*.

I am — I am ill too...

GOLAUD.

You, ill?... What is the matter, what
is the matter, Méli   de?...

MÉLISANDE.

I do not know... I am ill because of this
place... I must tell you now.   Prince,
prince, I am not happy here...

GOLAUD.

What has happened, Mélisande? What
is it?...   I had no idea of this...   What can
have happened?... Has any one harmed
you?... Has any one offended you?

MÉLISANDE.

No, no, no one has done me the slightest
harm... It is not that; not that. But I
cannot live here. I do not know why...
Would that I might go away, go away!...
I shall die if I stay here...

GOLAUD.

But something must have happened.
Are you concealing something from me?...
Tell me the whole truth, Mélisande... Is
it the king?... Is it my mother?... Is it
Pélléas?

MÉLISANDE.

No, no, it is not Pélléas. It is no one...
You do not understand me...

GOLAUD.

Why should I not understand?... If you
tell me nothing, what can I do for you?...
Tell me everything, and I shall understand
everything.

MÉLISANDE.

I know not what it is, myself... I cannot define it... If I could tell you I would
tell you... It is something stronger than
I am...

GOLAUD.

Come, be reasonable, Mélisande. — What can I do for you! — You are no longer a child. — Do you wish to leave me?

MÉLISANDE.

Oh, no, no, it is not that... I want to go away with you. I cannot live here any longer... If I do, I feel I shall soon die...

GOLAUD.

But there must be some reason. It seems like a child's freak, like madness... Let us see — Pélléas now — perhaps it is he. I think he does not often speak to you?...

MÉLISANDE.

Yes, yes, he speaks to me sometimes. I think he does not love me. I see it in his eyes... But he speaks to me when we meet...

GOLAUD.

You must not be offended with him. It has always been his way. He is a little odd, and he is sad now; his mind is running on his friend Marcellus, who is dying, and from whose bedside he has been kept.

He will be different, he will be different
by and by, you will find. He is young...

MÉLISANDE.

But it is not that... it is not that...

GOLAUD.

What is it, then ? — Can you not accom-
modate yourself to our life here ? Is it
too sad ? — It is true the castle is very old
and very gloomy. It is very cold and very
lonely. And all its inhabitants are old.
And the country may seem melancholy,
too, with all its forests, all its dark,
ancient forests. But we can brighten all
this. And then one cannot always be
joyful — we must take things as we find
them. But tell me anything that can be
done, no matter what. I will do anything
you wish...

MÉLISANDE.

Yes, yes, it is true... We never see the
sky here. I saw it for the first time this
morning !...

GOLAUD.

Then that is what makes you weep, my
poor Mélisande ? — Is it only that ? — Do

you weep because you cannot see the sky? — Come, come, you are too old to weep for such things... And, besides, is not summer coming? You can see the sky every day! — And then... next year... Come, give me your hand, give me both your little hands (*he takes her hands*). Oh, these little hands which I could crush like two flowers!... — Aha, where is the ring I gave you?

MÉLISANDE.

The ring?

GOLAUD.

Yes, our wedding-ring, where is it?

MÉLISANDE.

I think... I think it fell off...

GOLAUD.

Fell off? — Where did it fall? — You have not lost it?

MÉLISANDE.

No, no, it fell off... It must have fallen off... but I know where it is...

GOLAUD.

Where is it?

MÉLISANDE.

You know... you must know... the cave on the seashore.

GOLAUD.

Yes.

MÉLISANDE.

Well, it is there... It must be there... Yes, yes, I remember now... I went there this morning to gather shells for little Yniold... There are very pretty ones there... It slipped from my finger... then the tide came up, and I had to come away before I could find it.

GOLAUD.

Are you sure it is there?

MÉLISANDE.

Yes, yes, quite sure... I felt it slip and then all at once... the roar of the waves...

GOLAUD.

You must go at once and seek for it.

MÉLISANDE.

Must I go and seek for it at once?

GOLAUD.

Yes.

MÉLISANDE.

Now — immediately — in the darkness ?

GOLAUD.

Now immediately, in the darkness.
You must go at once and seek for it. I
would rather have lost everything I have
in the world than that ring. You know
not what it is. You know not whence it
came. The tide will be very high to-night.
The tide will get it before you... Hasten.
You must go and seek for it at once !...

MÉLISANDE.

I dare not... I dare not go alone.

GOLAUD.

Go, go, with any one. But go at once,
do you hear? — Hasten. Ask Pélléas to
go with you.

MÉLISANDE.

Pélléas ? — With Pélléas ? — But Pélléas
would not...

GOLAUD.

Pélléas will do anything you ask of him.
I know Pélléas better than you do. Go,
go. Hasten. I shall not sleep until I
have the ring.

MÉLISANDE.

Oh, I am so unhappy !... I am so unhappy !

(She goes out weeping.)

SCENE III.

BEFORE A CAVE.

(Enter Pélléas and Mélisande.)

PÉLLÉAS *(speaking very excitedly).*

Yes, it is here; we are in the place. It
is so dark that the entrance cannot be
seen in the blackness of the night... There
are no stars in this direction. Wait till
the moon breaks through that great cloud;
it will light up the cave, and then we can
enter safely. There are dangerous places,
and the path is very narrow, between two
deep and fathomless pools. It did not
occur to me to bring a torch or a lantern,
but I think the light of the moon may be
enough. — You have never gone into this
cave ?

MÉLISANDE.

No...

PÉLLÉAS.

Let us go in, let us go in... You must be able to describe the place where you lost the ring if he questions you... It is very deep and very beautiful. There are stalactites like trees and men. It is full of blue shadows. No one has ever explored its farthest recesses. Great treasures, it seems, were hidden here formerly. You will see the jetsam of old shipwrecks. But it will not be safe to go too far without a guide. Some who attempted it have never returned. I, myself, dare not go in too far. We will stop the moment the light of the moon or the sea fails us. If a little light were kindled, the vault above would seem to be as full of stars as the sky. They say the rock is gemmed with salt or crystals. — Come, come, I think the clouds are breaking... Give me your hand. Do not tremble, do not tremble so. There is no danger. We will stop the moment we lose the reflection from the sea... Is it the sound from the cave that frightens

"IT IS VERY DEEP AND VERY BEAUTIFUL."

you? It is the voice of the night or the voice of the silence... Do you hear the sea behind us? — It is disquieted to-night... Ah, there comes the moonlight!

(*The moon lights up the entrance and partially illuminates the darkness of the grotto, and at some distance within, three old white-haired beggars are seen seated side by side asleep against a ledge of rock.*)

MÉLISANDE.

Ah!

PÉLLÉAS.

What is it?

MÉLISANDE.

There — there!

(*She points to the three beggars.*)

PÉLLÉAS.

Yes, yes. I saw them too...

MÉLISANDE.

Let us go away!... Let us go away!...

PÉLLÉAS.

They are three old beggars who have gone to sleep there... There is a famine in the land... Why did they choose this place to sleep in?...

MÉLISANDE.

Let us go away !... Come, come !... Let us go away !

PÉLLÉAS.

Take care.   Do not speak so loud !... Let us not wake them... They still sleep profoundly... Come.

MÉLISANDE.

Let me go, let me go !   I prefer to walk alone...

PÉLLÉAS.

We will come again another time...

(They go out.)

SCENE IV.

AN APARTMENT IN THE CASTLE.

(Arkèl and Pélléas are discovered.)

ARKËL.

You see that everything keeps you here now, and that everything forbids your useless journey.   Your father's true condition has so far been concealed from you, but it is

probably hopeless, and that alone should
keep your foot from passing the threshold.
But there are many other reasons... And
at the moment when our enemies are wake-
ful and our people murmuring, and dying of
hunger about us, you have no right to
abandon us... Why take this journey at
all? Marcellus is dead, and life has
more important duties than a visit to a
tomb. You are tired, you say, of your in-
active life, but Activity and Duty are not
always best found abroad. They are to
be met at one's own door and compelled to
enter as they pass it, and each day they
pass ! Have you never seen them ? My own
old eyes are almost blind to them, but I will
teach you to see them, and I will point them
out to you when the time comes. And yet
— listen to me. If at the bottom of your
heart you believe in the necessity of this
journey, I do not forbid it, for you ought
to understand better than I the elements
which should form your life and shape your
destiny. I would only ask you to wait
until we know what is to happen — for a
little while...

PÉLLÉAS.

How long must I wait?

ARKËL.

A few weeks, perhaps only a few days

PÉLLÉAS.

I will wait...

ACT III.

SCENE I.

AN APARTMENT IN THE CASTLE.

(*Pélléas and Mélisande are discovered, Mélisande at her distaff at the back of the room.*)

PÉLLÉAS.

Yniold does not return! Where can he have gone?

MÉLISANDE.

He heard something in the corridor; he went to see what it was.

PÉLLÉAS.

Mélisande...

MÉLISANDE.

What is it?

PÉLLÉAS.

Can you see to work there ?

MÉLISANDE.

I can work quite as well in the dark.

PÉLLÉAS.

I believe the whole castle is asleep. Late as it is, Golaud has not returned from hunting... Does he still suffer from his fall ?

MÉLISANDE.

He says that he no longer suffers.

PÉLLÉAS.

He ought to be more careful. His body is not so elastic as when he was twenty... From the window I see the stars and the moonlight on the trees. It is late ; he will not come back. (*Some one knocks at the door.*) Who is there ?... Come in. (*Little Yniold opens the door and comes in.*) Is it you who knocked so loud ?... You ought not to knock in that way as though something was the matter. See how you have frightened mamma !

YNIOLD.

Indeed I only knocked very softly.

PÉLLÉAS.

It is late. Papa will not come back to-night. It is time for you to go to bed.

YNIOLD.

I will not go to bed before you do.

PÉLLÉAS.

What ?... What did you say ?

YNIOLD.

I said... not before you do — not before you do...

(*He bursts into tears and runs to Mélisande.*)

MÉLISANDE.

What is it, Yniold ?... What is it ?... Why do you cry so, all at once ?

YNIOLD (*sobbing*).

Because... oh ! oh !... because...

MÉLISANDE.

Why ?... why ?... Tell me...

YNIOLD.

Mamma... mamma... you are going away !...

MÉLISANDE.

What ails you, Yniold ?... I have never thought of going away...

YNIOLD.

Yes, yes ; papa has gone... papa will not come back and you are going too... I know it... I know it...

MÉLISANDE.

But no one ever dreamed of such a thing, Yniold... What made you think I was going ?...

YNIOLD.

I know... I know... You told my uncle things I was not meant to hear...

PÉLLÉAS.

He is so sleepy... he has been dreaming. Come here, Yniold — or are you quite asleep ? Come here to the window and see the swans attacking the dogs...

YNIOLD (*at the window*).

Oh, they are chasing the dogs !... They are chasing them — right into the water !... How they flap their great wings !... The dogs are frightened...

PÉLLÉAS (*approaching Mélisande once more*).

He is sleepy ; though he is struggling so hard, his eyes are almost shut...

MÉLISANDE (*singing low as she spins*).
" Saint Daniel and Saint Michael,
    Saint Michael and Saint Raphael."

YNIOLD (*at the window*).
Oh, mamma, mamma !

MÉLISANDE (*rising hastily*).
What is it, Yniold ?... what is it ?...

YNIOLD.
I saw something at the window.
(*Pélléas and Mélisande go hastily to the window.*)

PÉLLÉAS.
What is at the window ?... What did you see ?

YNIOLD.
Oh, I saw — I saw something...

PÉLLÉAS.
But there is nothing. I can see nothing...

MÉLISANDE.

Nor I...

PÉLLÉAS.

Where did you think you saw it? In which direction?...

YNIOLD.

Down there... down there... 'Tis gone!...

PÉLLÉAS.

He does not know what he is saying. He might have seen a moonbeam through the trees. They often fall weirdly in the forest... or else something passed along the road... or he dreamed it all, for see, see, I believe he is really asleep...

YNIOLD (*at the window*).

Papa is there! papa is there!

PÉLLÉAS (*going to the window*).

He is right. Golaud is just entering the courtyard...

YNIOLD.

Papa... papa!... I'm going to meet him...
(*He runs out. — Silence.*)

PÉLLÉAS.

They are coming up the staircase...

(*Enter Golaud and little Yniold, who carries a lamp.*)

GOLAUD.

You are still waiting in darkness?

YNIOLD.

I have brought a light, mamma, a big light!... (*He holds up the lamp and looks at Mélisande.*) You have been weeping, mamma... You have been weeping!... (*He holds the lamp towards Pélléas, and looks at him in turn.*) You have been weeping, too!... Papa, look, papa, they have both been weeping!...

GOLAUD.

Don't dazzle their eyes so with the light.

SCENE II.

ONE OF THE TOWERS OF THE CASTLE. — A
WINDING STAIRCASE PASSES UNDER A
WINDOW OF THE TOWER.

MÉLISANDE (*at the window combing her
hair, which falls loose about her.*)

My long, long locks unplaited
  Unto the ground they fall;
My locks for you have waited
  As long as the length of the wall,
    And all day long they call,
    And all day long they call...

Saint Daniel and Saint Michael,
Saint Michael and Saint Raphael.

My birthday was a Sunday,
All on a Sunday noon.

(*Enter Pélléas by the winding staircase.*)

PÉLLÉAS.

Hist !   Hallo !   Ho !...

MÉLISANDE.

Who is there ?

PÉLLÉAS.

I, 'tis I — Pélléas !... What are you doing there, singing at the window like a beautiful strange bird ?

MÉLISANDE.

I was putting up my hair for the night...

PÉLLÉAS.

Is it your hair that I see against the wall ?... I thought you had a light there...

MÉLISANDE.

I had to open the window. It was so warm within... It is lovely to-night...

PÉLLÉAS.

There are innumerable stars. I never saw so many as there are to-night... but the moon has not risen yet above the sea... Do not stay so far back, Mélisande ; lean over a little that I may see your hair unbound...

MÉLISANDE.

I am not fit to be seen so !...

(*She leans from the window.*)

PÉLLÉAS.

Oh ! Mélisande !... oh ! how beautiful you

are thus... how beautiful!...   Lean, lean
toward me !... let me come closer to you...

MÉLISANDE.

I cannot come any closer to you...   I am
leaning as far toward you as I can...

PÉLLÉAS.

I can get no higher... Give me your
hand this one night before I go...   I am
going to-morrow...

MÉLISANDE.

No, no, no !...

PÉLLÉAS.

Yes, yes, yes ! I go — and I go to-morrow...   Give me your hand, your hand,
your little hand, that for once I may press
it to my lips...

MÉLISANDE.

I will not give you my hand, if you go
away...

PÉLLÉAS.

Give it me, oh, give it me !...

MÉLISANDE.

And you will not go ?...

PÉLLÉAS.
I will stay — I will stay...

MÉLISANDE.
I see a rose in the shadow there...

PÉLLÉAS.
Where?... I see only the branches of the willow drooping over the wall...

MÉLISANDE.
Lower, lower, down there in the garden in those deep-green shadows...

PÉLLÉAS.
It is not a rose... I will go and look for it presently, but give me your hand first— first your hand!...

MÉLISANDE.
There, there!... I cannot lean down any farther...

PÉLLÉAS.
I cannot reach your hand with my lips.

MÉLISANDE.
I cannot lean down any farther. I am almost falling... Oh, oh! there goes all my hair!

(Her hair suddenly falls forward as she leans out, and envelops Pélléas.)

PÉLLÉAS.

Ah, what is this !...   Your hair, your hair has fallen over me...   All your hair, Mélisande, all your hair has enveloped me...   I am folding it in my hands.   I press it to my lips...   I embrace it.   I wrap it round my neck.   I will hold it all night long...

MÉLISANDE.

Let me go!   Let me go !...   You will make me fall !...

PÉLLÉAS.

No, no, no !...   I never saw such hair as yours, Mélisande !...   See, see, though you are so far above me, it reaches to my heart — it reaches to my knees.   And it is sweet, sweet as though it fell from heaven...   I cannot see the sky through the flood of hair.   Do you see, do you see ?...   My two hands cannot hold it all; it is caught in the willow branches...   Your tresses are like living birds in my hands ;... and they love me, they love me more than you do !...

"I NEVER SAW SUCH HAIR AS YOURS, MÉLISANDE!"

MÉLISANDE.

Let me go, let me go !... Some one might come.

PÉLLÉAS.

No, no, no; I will not let you go to-night... You are my prisoner to-night; all night, all night...

MÉLISANDE.

Pélléas, Pélléas !...

PÉLLÉAS.

I tie your locks, I tie them to the branches. You cannot get away... You cannot get away... Look! look! I kiss your hair... I no longer feel any sorrow while it surrounds me... Do you hear my kisses on it?... They climb up your tresses... Each one shall carry up my kisses to you... You see, you see; I release you with my hands... My hands are free; and yet you cannot leave me.

MÉLISANDE.

Oh! oh! you hurt me... (*Doves come from the tower and fly about them in the darkness.*) What is it, Pélléas ?—What is flying about me ?

PÉLLÉAS.

They are doves coming out of the tower... I have frightened them. They are flying away...

MÉLISANDE.

They are my doves, Pélléas. You must leave me. Let me go ! They would never come back !...

PÉLLÉAS.

Why do you think they would not come back ?

MÉLISANDE.

They will lose their way in the darkness... Let me go, let me raise my head... I hear a step... It is Golaud !... It must be Golaud. He has overheard us !...

PÉLLÉAS.

Wait ! Wait !... Your hair is wound around the branches... It is caught there in the darkness. Wait, wait !... I cannot see !...

(*Enter Golaud by the winding stair.*)

GOLAUD.

What are you doing here ?

PÉLLÉAS.

What am I doing ?... I...

GOLAUD.

You are children... Mélisande, do not lean so far out of window. You will fall... Do you not know how late it is ? — It is after midnight — How foolish to play in this way in the dark !... You are a pair of children *(laughing nervously).* A pair of children.

(He goes out with Pélléas.)

SCENE III.

THE VAULTS OF THE CASTLE.

(Enter Golaud and Pélléas.)

GOLAUD.

Take care ! This way, this way. — You have never been into these underground vaults ?

PÉLLÉAS.

Yes, once upon a time, but it was long ago...

GOLAUD.

They are monstrous in size; there is a series of enormous crypts ending, heaven knows where! The whole castle is built over these vaults. Do you smell the death odor here? — That is what I wanted you to perceive. I believe it arises from the little subterranean lake I am going to show you. Take care, walk before me where the light of my lantern falls. I will let you know when we are there. (*They walk on in silence.*) Ah, ha, Pélléas, stop, stop. (*He seizes his arm.*) Great heaven!... Do you not see? — Another step and you would have been in the gulf!...

PÉLLÉAS.

I did not see... The light of the lantern disappeared all at once...

GOLAUD.

I made a misstep... But if I had not caught your arm!... Well, here is the stagnant water of which I was speaking to you... Do you perceive the odor of death rising?... Let us go to the edge of this overhanging rock, and do you lean over a little way. You will feel it in your face.

PÉLLÉAS.

I smell it already... It is like the stench from a tomb.

GOLAUD.

Farther — farther... This it is which poisons the air of the whole castle sometimes. The king will not believe it comes from here. — This grotto of stagnant water should be walled up. It would be well, also, to examine these vaults. Did you notice these fissures in the walls and the pillars which sustain the arches ? — No one suspects the decay which is going on here. The whole castle will be swallowed up some day, if something is not done. But no one likes to comes to this place... There are strange cracks in many of the walls... Here again ... do you perceive the deathly odor rising ?

PÉLLÉAS.

Yes ; there is a deathly odor rising round us here...

GOLAUD.

Lean over; have no fear... I will hold
you... give me... no, no, not your hand, it
might slip... your arm, your arm!   Do
you see straight down into the abyss?
(*Anxiously*) Pélléas! Pélléas!...

PÉLLÉAS.

Yes, I fancy I can see to the bottom of
the abyss...   Is it the light which is trem-
bling?...   Golaud!...

(*He stands up, turns and looks intently
at Golaud.*)

GOLAUD (*in a tremulous voice*).

Yes, it is the lantern... See, I was moving it so as to throw light upon the walls...

PÉLLÉAS.

I am stifling here... Let us go!

GOLAUD.

Yes; let us go.

(*They go out in silence.*)

"IS IT YOU, GRANDFATHER?"

"AH! I BREATHE ONCE MORE."

SCENE IV.

A TERRACE WITHOUT THE VAULTS.

(Enter Golaud and Pélléas.)

PÉLLÉAS.

Ah! I breathe once more... I thought
for a moment I should be ill in those enormous vaults. I almost fell... The air there
is damp and heavy, like a leaden dew, and
the darkness thick, like poisoned slime. —
And now, air, the pure air, of the open
sea!... See how fresh the wind is, fresh as
a new-opened leaf of the spring foliage...
Hold! Some one has just been watering
the flowers below the terrace, and the fra-
grance of dewy roses and verdure is wafted
up... It must be near noon, as they are
even now in the shadow of the tower... It
is noon! I hear the clocks striking twelve,
and the children are going to the shore to
bathe... I did not think we had been so
long in the vaults...

GOLAUD.

We went down towards eleven...

PÉLLÉAS.

Earlier; it must have been earlier. I
heard the half-stroke after ten.

GOLAUD.

Half-past ten or a quarter to eleven...

PÉLLÉAS.

All the windows of the castle are open.
It will be very warm this afternoon...
There is our mother and Mélisande at one
of the tower windows...

GOLAUD.

Yes; they are in the shade on that side.
— About Mélisande: I overheard what
passed, and what was said last night. I
understand quite well that it was only
child's play, but it must not be repeated.
Mélisande is very young and very im-
pressionable, and it is necessary to be
more than usually careful, as she is with
child, we think... She is very delicate;
still a mere girl, and the least emotion
might be serious. It is not the first time
that I have noticed something between
you... You are much older than she is,
and so I speak to you. I have said enough

in saying this... Avoid her as much as possible, but without affectation, without affectation... — What is it I see in the forest road ?

PÉLLÉAS.

Flocks, driven to the town...

GOLAUD.

They cry like lost children. One might think they already smelled the butcher's knife ! — It is time to go to dinner. — What a beautiful day ! What perfect harvest weather !...

(They go out.)

SCENE   V.

BEFORE THE CASTLE.

(Enter Golaud and little Yniold.)

GOLAUD.

Come, let us sit here, Yniold. I will take you on my lap ; we can see from here what is going on in the forest. I have not seen you at all for a long time. You have de-

serted me like the rest. You are always
with mamma... See, we are just under
mamma's window now. — Perhaps at this
moment she is saying her prayers... But
tell me, Yniold, she is a great deal with
your uncle Pélléas, is she not ?

YNIOLD.

Yes, yes, papa, always — when you are
not there, papa...

GOLAUD.

Ah ! — Wait a moment. There goes
some one with a lantern in the garden. —
But I thought they did not like each other...
I was told that they quarrelled often — is
it not so ?

YNIOLD.

Yes, yes, it's true.

GOLAUD.

Do they ? — Ah, ha ! — But what do
they quarrel about ?

YNIOLD.

About the door.

GOLAUD.

What do you mean ? — about the door ?

What are you talking about ? — Explain what you mean — why do they quarrel about the door ?

YNIOLD.

Because it cannot be open.

GOLAUD.

Who does not wish it open ? — Come, tell me why do they quarrel ?

YNIOLD.

I do not know, papa, — about the light.

GOLAUD.

Never mind the light; we will talk of that presently. We were talking about the door. Answer distinctly what I ask you; you are old enough to reply to a plain question... Don't put your fingers into your mouth. Come...

YNIOLD.

Papa, papa !... I won't do it again. (*He bursts into tears.*)

GOLAUD.

Come, come, what are you crying for now ? What is the matter ?

YNIOLD.

Oh, oh, papa, you hurt me !...

GOLAUD.

Did I hurt you ? — Where did I hurt you ?   I did not mean to do so...

YNIOLD.

Here, here; on my little arm...

GOLAUD.

It was an accident; come, do not cry any more.   I will give you something to-morrow...

YNIOLD.

What, papa ?

GOLAUD.

A quiver and some arrows; but tell me what you know about the door.

YNIOLD.

Big arrows ?

GOLAUD.

Yes, yes, big arrows. — But why do they not want the door open ?   See, you must and shall answer ! — No, don't open your mouth to cry.   I am not angry.   We will talk as peaceably as Pélléas and mamma do when they are together. What do they talk about when they are together?

YNIOLD.

Pélléas and mamma?

GOLAUD.

Yes, what do they talk of?

YNIOLD.

Me, nothing but me.

GOLAUD.

And what do they say of you?

YNIOLD.

They say that I am going to be very tall.

GOLAUD.

Ah, miserable man that I am!... I am like a blind man seeking for a lost treasure at the bottom of the sea!... I am like an infant lost in a forest — and you... But listen, Yniold, I was wandering. We were going to talk quite seriously. Do Pélléas and mamma never speak of me when I am not there?...

YNIOLD.

Yes, papa, oh, yes; they are always talking about you.

GOLAUD.

Ah !... and what do they say of me ?

YNIOLD.

They say I shall grow up as tall as you.

GOLAUD.

Are you always near them ?

YNIOLD.

Yes, yes, always, papa.

GOLAUD.

Do they never tell you to go and play somewhere else ?

YNIOLD.

No, papa. They are afraid when I am not with them.

GOLAUD.

They are afraid ?... How do you know they are afraid ?

YNIOLD.

Mamma says always : " Don't go. Don't go away ! "... They are unhappy, though they try to smile...

GOLAUD.

But that does not show they are afraid.

YNIOLD.

Yes, papa, she is afraid...

GOLAUD.

Why do you say that she is afraid?

YNIOLD.

They are always weeping when it is dark.

GOLAUD.

Ah, ha!...

YNIOLD.

That makes me cry, too...

GOLAUD.

Yes, yes...

YNIOLD.

And she is so pale, papa.

GOLAUD.

Oh, my God... patience, give me patience!...

YNIOLD.

What did you say, papa?

GOLAUD.

Nothing, nothing, child, — I saw a wolf go by in the forest. — Then they understand each other? — I am glad to know

they agree so well. Do they ever kiss
each other ? — Eh ?...

YNIOLD.

Do they kiss each other, papa ? — No,
no, — oh, yes, I remember once, once when
he was weeping !...

GOLAUD.

They kissed each other ? — But how was
it, tell me how ! Tell me ! —

YNIOLD.

Why, this way, papa, this way. (*He
kisses Golaud's mouth, laughing.*) Oh,
your beard, papa ! It pricks ! It pricks !
It is getting all gray, papa ; and your
hair too, all gray, all gray, all gray... (*The
window under which they are sitting is
lighted up, and the light falls upon them.*)
Oh, oh, mamma has lit her lamp ! How
light it makes it, papa ! how light !...

GOLAUD.

Yes, it begins to grow light...

YNIOLD.

Let us go in there too, papa, let us go...

GOLAUD.
Where do you want to go ?

YNIOLD.
Where the light is, papa !

GOLAUD.
No, no, my child, let us stay here in the shadow a little while... I do not know enough yet, not yet... Do you see those beggars down there who have been vainly trying to light a little fire in the wood ? — It has been raining. And over there, do you see the old gardener attempting to raise the tree which the wind blew down across the road ? — He cannot ; the tree is too large ; the tree is too heavy ; it must lie where it fell. There is no help for such things... I think Pélléas is mad !

YNIOLD.
No, papa, he is not mad, he is very good.

GOLAUD.
Do you want to see mamma ?

YNIOLD.
Oh, yes, I want to see her.

GOLAUD.

Make no noise. I will lift you up to
the window. It is too high for me, tall as
I am... (*He lifts Yniold to his shoulder.*)
Don't make the slightest noise, mamma
would be terribly frightened... Do you
see her ? — Is she in the room ?

YNIOLD.

Yes.   Oh! how light it is !

GOLAUD.

Is she alone ?

YNIOLD.

Yes...   No, no; my uncle Pélléas is
there too.

GOLAUD.

He !...

YNIOLD.

Oh, papa, you hurt me !...

GOLAUD.

No matter, be quiet. I will not do it
again. Look, look, Yniold !...   I only
stumbled ! Speak lower. What are they
doing ? —

YNIOLD.

They are doing nothing, papa; they are waiting for something.

GOLAUD.

Are they near each other?

YNIOLD.

No, papa.

GOLAUD.

And... and the bed? Are they near the bed?

YNIOLD.

The bed, papa? — I don't see the bed.

GOLAUD.

Lower, speak lower, they will hear you. Are they talking?

YNIOLD.

No, papa, they are not talking.

GOLAUD.

But what are they doing? — They must be doing something...

YNIOLD.

They are looking at the light.

GOLAUD.

Both of them?

YNIOLD.

Yes, papa.

GOLAUD.

Are they still silent?

YNIOLD.

Yes, papa; they are just staring.

GOLAUD.

Do they not come toward each other?

YNIOLD.

No, papa; they do not stir.

GOLAUD.

Are they sitting down?

YNIOLD.

No, papa; they are leaning against the wall.

GOLAUD.

Do they make no motion? — Do they not look at each other? — Do they make no signs?...

YNIOLD. .

No, papa. — Oh, papa, they never close their eyes!... I am terribly frightened!...

GOLAUD.

Be quiet. Do they not move yet?

YNIOLD.

No, papa ! — I'm afraid, papa. — Let me down ! Let me down !...

GOLAUD.

What are you afraid of ? — Look ! look !...

YNIOLD.

I dare not look any longer, papa !... Let me down !...

GOLAUD.

Look ! look !...

YNIOLD.

Oh, I shall not be able to help crying out loud, papa ! — Let me down, let me down !...

GOLAUD.

Well, then, we will go and see what has happened.

(They go out.)

ACT IV.

SCENE I.

A CORRIDOR IN THE CASTLE.

(*Pélléas and Mélisande enter, meeting.*)

PÉLLÉAS.

Where are you going ?   I must speak to
you to-night.   May I see you ?

MÉLISANDE.

Yes.

PÉLLÉAS.

I have just left my father's bedside. He
is better ; the doctor tells us he will recover
now...   And yet I had a presentiment only
this morning that some misfortune would
happen to-day. I have had for a long
time a sense of impending evil... Now
there is suddenly a great change ; it is

only a question of time. They have
opened all his windows. He talks; he
seems happy. He does not talk like an
ordinary man yet, but his thoughts no
longer seem to come from another world...
He knew me; he pressed my hand and said
with that air of solemnity which his illness
has given him, "Is it you, Pélléas? I never
saw in you before that grave and wistful
look which belongs to those whose days are
numbered... You must have some change
— you must travel..." It is strange. I must
obey him... My mother, who was standing
by, wept for joy. — Have you not felt the
difference in everything? — The whole
house seems to breathe freely with a new
life, every one speaks and walks differ-
ently... Hark! there are people talking
outside of that door. Quick, quick, tell me
quick, where may I see you?

MÉLISANDE.
Where do you wish me to come?

PÉLLÉAS.
To the park, by the Fountain of the
Blind. — Will you? — Will you come?

MÉLISANDE.

Yes.

PÉLLÉAS.

It will be the last evening. — I am going away as my father has ordered me. You will not see me again...

MÉLISANDE.

Do not say that, Pélléas... I shall see you always. I shall always look to you...

PÉLLÉAS.

You will look in vain... I shall be too far away for you to see me... I shall go as far as possible... I am very happy to-day and I feel as if I had all the weight of earth and heaven on me to-day...

MÉLISANDE.

What has happened, Pélléas? — I do not understand you...

PÉLLÉAS.

We must part ; go now — go ! I hear voices outside that door... They must be the strangers who came to the castle this morning and are leaving now... Let us go ! They are the strangers...

      (*They go out in opposite directions.*)

SCENE II.

AN APARTMENT IN THE CASTLE.

(Arkël and Mélisande discovered.)

ARKËL.

Now that Pélléas's father is out of danger
and that Death's dismal familiar, Illness,
has left the castle, some joy and some sunshine may come back to the house at last...
It's time ! — Since you came to us we have
all been whispering round a sick man's
chamber... and truly I have pitied you,
Mélisande !... You came to us joyous as a
child summoned to a festival, and from the
moment you crossed the threshold I saw
your face change, and I think your spirit fell
too in spite of you, as one who, from the
cheerful noonday, enters suddenly a cold,
dark cave... And since then, since then, it
was probably that which has made you so
incomprehensible to me... I watched you.
You were here, unconscious, perhaps, but
seeming bewildered and frightened, like
one who even in a bright garden in the
sunshine might shiver with a feeling of

some coming misery... I cannot explain
my feeling... But it has saddened me to
see you thus ; for you are too young and
too beautiful to dwell night and day under
the shadow of death... Now everything
will be different. Now that I am so very
old I can see the great lesson of my long
life has been the faith I have learned in
the justice of events, and I have always
noted that every young and beautiful creature attracts to itself fresh, happy, and
beautiful conditions... So you shall be
leader in the new life we are to enjoy.
Come to me ; why do you stand mute with
downcast eyes ? — I have never kissed you
once since the day of your arrival, and yet
the old need sometimes to touch with their
lips a woman's forehead or a child's cheek,
that they may still believe in the promise
of life and forget for a moment its sad
omens... Do you dread my old lips ?
How I have pitied you all these long
months !...

MÉLISANDE.

Grandfather, I have not been unhappy...

ARKËL.

Perhaps you were one of those who are unhappy without knowing it... and those are the most unhappy of all!... Let me keep you here and let me look at you a moment... Living beauty is so precious to one who stands near the grave!...

(Enter Golaud.)

GOLAUD.

Pélléas starts to-night.

ARKËL.

There is blood on your forehead. — What has happened?

GOLAUD.

Nothing, nothing... I passed through a thicket of thorn bushes.

MÉLISANDE.

Bend down your head, prince... I will wipe your forehead...

GOLAUD *(repulsing her)*.

Do not touch me. Do you hear? Out with you! — I do not wish to speak to you. — Where is my sword? — I came for my sword...

MÉLISANDE.

Here ; on the prie-Dieu !

GOLAUD.

Give it me. (*To Arkël.*) They have just
found another peasant dead of starvation,
by the seashore.   It would seem as if they
all chose to die here under our eyes. — (*To
Mélisande.*) Well, where is my sword ? —
Why do you tremble so ? — I do not intend
to kill you.   I only want to examine the
blade.   I do not use my sword for such
purposes.   Why do you stare at me as
though I were a beggar ? — I have asked
no alms from you.   Do you expect to read
my eyes while you prevent my reading
yours ? — Do you suppose I know anything ? — (*To Arkèl.*) Do you see those
beautiful eyes ? — They seem to glory in
their power...

ARKËL.

I only see how innocent they are...

GOLAUD.

Innocent ? — They are more than innocent.   They are purer than the eyes of a
lamb...   They might teach their Creator a

"DOWN ON YOUR KNEES!"

lesson of innocence. Innocent! Hear me!
I am so near them that I can feel the
freshness of their lids as they close, and
yet I know less of the mighty secrets of
the other world than the least secret those
eyes could disclose... Innocent?... More
than innocent! Their tears are like the
dew of an angelic baptism... I know those
eyes. I have seen their work. Close
them, close them, or I will close them forever!...— You need not put your right hand
to your neck. I have said a very simple
thing... I have no concealed meaning. —
Why should I not say everything I mean?
Ah — don't try to escape! — Here! — give
me this hand.— Your hands are too warm...
Away! The touch of your flesh disgusts
me... Here! — you shall not escape me
now! — (*He seizes her by the hair.*) —Down
on your knees. — On your knees!— Down
on your knees to me! — Ah, your long hair
is of some use now! — This way, and now
that. — That way, and this again. — Absalom! Absalom!— Forward, now back!—
To the ground, I say... Ha! ha! You see,
you see, I am imbecile already!...

ARKËL (*running to stop Golaud*).
Golaud !...

GOLAUD (*affecting suddenly disdainful calmness*).
You are free to act as you wish. — It is of no consequence to me. — I am much too old to care... I am not a spy. I will await my opportunity, and if it comes — oh then... why, then I shall only act as custom demands ! as custom demands !...

(*He goes out.*)

ARKËL.
What is the matter ? — Is he sober ?

MÉLISANDE (*in tears*).
Yes, yes, but he hates me — and I am so wretched !... so wretched !...

ARKËL.
If I were God, how infinitely I should pity the hearts of men !...

SCENE III.

A TERRACE OF THE CASTLE.

(*Yniold is discovered trying to raise a great rock.*)

YNIOLD.

Oh, how heavy this stone is !... It is heavier than I am !... It is heavier than the whole world... It is heavier than all that ever was made... I see my shiny ball between the rock and this wicked stone, but I cannot reach it... My little arm is not long enough... and this stone will not be moved... I cannot stir it, and no one on earth can... It is heavier than the whole castle... it must have roots in the ground. (*The distant bleating of sheep is heard.*) Oh, oh, I hear the sheep crying ! (*He looks over the edge of the terrace.*) Oh ! the sun has gone in... There come the sheep ! There they come !... What a lot of them there are ! What a lot of them there are !... They are afraid of the dark... How they huddle together ! They can scarcely get along... How they cry ! And now they

are scampering so fast! They are at the
crossways, and they know not which
way to turn... They cry no more. They
hesitate... Some want to go to the
right... Now they are all trying to go to
the right... He will not let them. The
shepherd knocks them about and throws
some down with his stick... Ah, they are
coming this way... They obey, they obey!
They will pass by the terrace under the
cliff... I shall see them close!... How many
there are!— how many! The whole road
is full of them. Now they are all quiet
again... Shepherd. why don't they speak
any more?

SHEPHERD (*below*).

Because they are going away from the
fold.

YNIOLD.

Where are they going? — Shepherd,
shepherd!— Where are they going? —
He does not hear me. They are too far
off... They are going quickly now... They
make no noise... They are going away
from the fold?— Where will they sleep

to-night? — Oh, how dark it is getting!
I must find somebody to speak to!...

(Runs out.)

SCENE IV.

A FOUNTAIN IN THE PARK.

(Enter Pélléas.)

PÉLLÉAS.

It is the last time... the last time...
Everything shall be ended... I have been
playing, like a child, with what I did not
suspect... playing close to the snares of
Fate... What is it that has caused this
sudden waking? I am flying as a blind
man might fly, who had set his house in
flames, with a heart bursting at once with
joy and pain... I will tell her that I am
going... My father is out of danger, and I
can no longer lie to myself with that
excuse... It is late; she is not coming...
It would be better that I should go without seeing her again... But I must look at
her closely this once... There are many
little things I cannot recall... It seems a

hundred years since I saw her last, somehow... And I have not yet looked deep
into her eyes... I shall be empty indeed if
I go thus unsatisfied. All my sweet mem-
ories, they are like water, carried away
in a muslin bag!... I must see her one
last time. I must see the bottom of her
heart... And I must tell her all I have not
said...

(Enter Mélisande.)

MÉLISANDE.

Pélléas.

PÉLLÉAS.

Mélisande! — Is it you, Mélisande?

MÉLISANDE.

Yes!

PÉLLÉAS.

Come here, out of the moonlight. —
Come here. We have much to say to
each other... Come here, under the shade
of the linden.

MÉLISANDE.

Let me stay in the moonlight...

PÉLLÉAS.

They might see us from the windows of

the tower. Come here; here where there
is no danger. Take care; they might see
us there...

MÉLISANDE.

I wish to be seen...

PÉLLÉAS.

What do you mean ? — You came out
unperceived surely ?

MÉLISANDE.

Yes, your brother was asleep.

PÉLLÉAS.

It is late. — In an hour the doors will
be shut. We must be careful. Why did
you come so late ?

MÉLISANDE.

Your brother had a bad dream. Then
my gown caught in the door. See, it is
torn. Then, as I had lost so much time, I
ran !...

PÉLLÉAS.

My poor Mélisande !... I am almost
afraid to touch you... You are still panting
like a hunted bird... Is it for me you did
this — you ran so ?... I hear the beating

of your heart as though it were my own...
Come here... near — nearer me...

MÉLISANDE.

Why do you laugh ?

PÉLLÉAS.

I was not laughing... or else perhaps I
did laugh for joy without knowing it...
Perhaps there were better reason to weep!

MÉLISANDE.

We   have   been   here   before...   I remember...

PÉLLÉAS.

Yes... yes... Long months ago. — I did
not know then... Do you know why I
asked you to come to-night ?

MÉLISANDE.

No.

PÉLLÉAS.

Perhaps this is the last time I shall ever
see you...   I must go — and forever...

MÉLISANDE.

Why do you always tell me that you
must go away ?...

PÉLLÉAS.

Must I tell you what you already know ? — Do you not know what I am going to say ?

MÉLISANDE.

No, no, I do not know at all...

PÉLLÉAS.

You do not know why I must go !... You do not know it is because ... (*He kisses her passionately*) I love you !...

MÉLISANDE (*in a low voice*).

And I love you also !...

PÉLLÉAS.

Oh ! what did you say, Mélisande ?... I scarcely heard it !... The ice is melted with glowing fire !... Your voice seemed to come from the ends of the earth !... I scarcely heard it at all !... You love me ? — You love me also ?— Since when, Mélisande ?

MÉLISANDE.

Always — always — when I saw you first...

PÉLLÉAS.

Oh, what divine words !... Your voice is

like the soft south wind which breathes
over the ocean in springtime... I never
heard a voice so sweet... Now it makes
my heart weep for joy!... And you tell it
to me so simply !... Like the response
of an angel... I cannot believe it, Mélisande!... Why should you love me ? —
Why do you love me ? — Is it true ? — You
are not deceiving me ? You have not been
saying what is not wholly true in order to
make me happy ?...

MÉLISANDE.

No, I always speak the truth to you ; I
only lie to your brother...

PÉLLÉAS.

Oh, how you speak! Your voice ! — Your
voice !...   It is fresher and clearer than falling water...   It is like pure water on my
lips !...   It is like pure water on my hands...
Give me, give me your hands... How small
these hands are !...   I did not know how
beautiful you were !...   I have never seen
anything so beautiful !...   I was unquiet,
seeking everywhere at home and seeking everywhere abroad — I never found

beauty... And now I have found thee... I have found thee! I do not believe there is a more beautiful creature upon earth... Where are you? — I can no longer hear you breathe!...

MÉLISANDE.

I am looking up into your face...

PÉLLÉAS.

Why do you look at me so solemnly? — We are in the shadow now. — It is too dark under this tree. Come into the light. We cannot see how happy we are! Come, come; so brief a time remains to us!...

MÉLISANDE.

No, no, let us stay here... I feel nearer you in the darkness...

PÉLLÉAS.

Where are your eyes? — You are not going to flee from me? — You are not thinking of me now!

MÉLISANDE.

Yes, yes, indeed. I am thinking only of you...

PÉLLÉAS.

Your eyes are far away...

MÉLISANDE.

I still see you there.

PÉLLÉAS.

Your thoughts are wandering — What is the matter? — You seem unhappy!...

MÉLISANDE.

Oh, no, I am happy — yet I am sad!...

PÉLLÉAS.

Those who love are often sad...

MÉLISANDE.

I always weep when I think of you...

PÉLLÉAS.

And I, too... I, too, Mélisande... Even now, near as I am to you, I weep for joy. (*He kisses her again.*)... It is so strange when I kiss you so... You are so beautiful that one might fear you had not long to live.

MÉLISANDE.

And you also...

PÉLLÉAS.

We do not what we will to do... I did
not love you when first.... I saw you...

MÉLISANDE.

Nor I, nor I... I was afraid...

PÉLLÉAS.

I could not endure your eyes... I wished
at first to avoid them... and then...

MÉLISANDE.

I dreaded to come here... Even now
I know not why, but I was afraid to come...

PÉLLÉAS.

There are so many things that we shall
never know... We wait, and then... What
is that noise ? — They are closing the doors.

MÉLISANDE.

Yes, the doors are shut...

PÉLLÉAS.

We cannot return ! — Do you hear the
locks turn ? — Listen ! Listen !... And now
the bolts and bars ?... It is too late, too
late !...

"THERE IS SOME ONE BEHIND US."

MÉLISANDE.

So much the better! So much the better!...

PÉLLÉAS.

Do you say that?... Well, it is no longer our doing... All is lost, but all is gained, all is gained to-night!—Come, come... My heart throbs madly, it is stifling me! (*He strains her to him.*) Listen, listen, my heart is bursting. — Come, come!... Ah! how beautiful it is in the darkness here!...

MÉLISANDE.

There is some one behind us...

PÉLLÉAS.

I see no one...

MÉLISANDE.

I heard a noise...

PÉLLÉAS.

I only hear your heart beating in the darkness...

MÉLISANDE.

I heard the dead leaves crackling...

PÉLLÉAS.

It is the wind which suddenly stirs

again... It fell when you were in my
arms...

MÉLISANDE.

What long shadows we have to-night...

PÉLLÉAS.

They are entwined to the very bottom
of the garden... See how they embrace
each other far from us!... Look! look!...

MÉLISANDE *(in a choked voice)*.

A-a-h! He is behind a tree!

PÉLLÉAS.

Who?

MÉLISANDE.

Golaud!

PÉLLÉAS.

Golaud? — Where? — I see nothing....

MÉLISANDE.

There...beyond our shadows...

PÉLLÉAS.

Yes, yes, I saw him then... We must
not move too suddenly...

MÉLISANDE.

He has his sword.

PÉLLÉAS.

And I have none !

MÉLISANDE.

He must have seen me in your arms !...

PÉLLÉAS.

He does not know we have seen him...
Do not stir, do not turn your head. He
might rush upon us !...   He will remain
there as long as he thinks he is unperceived ; he is watching us...   He is motion-
less still...   Go, go this way at once,
now !...   I will wait for him !...   I will
hold him back...

MÉLISANDE.

No, no, no !...

PÉLLÉAS.

Go, go !   He has seen everything...   He
will kill us !

MÉLISANDE.

So much the better !   So much the
better !..

PÉLLÉAS.

He is coming !   He is coming !...   Your
mouth — your mouth !...

MÉLISANDE.

Yes! yes! yes! (*They kiss each other desperately.*)

PÉLLÉAS.

Oh, all the stars are falling from heaven!...

MÉLISANDE.

And on me, on me also!...

PÉLLÉAS.

Again, give me, give me — more!...

MÉLISANDE.

All — everything!

(*Golaud rushes forward with drawn sword, and hews down Pélléas, who falls by the fountain. Mélisande flees in terror.*)

MÉLISANDE (*escaping*).

Oh, coward that I am... My courage is all gone!

(*Golaud silently pursues her into the forest.*)

ACT V.

SCENE I.

A LOWER HALL IN THE CASTLE.

(*The maid-servants are discovered.   Outside, children playing are seen through grated windows.*)

AN AGED SERVING-WOMAN.

You will see, you will see, my children. It is to be to-night. — We shall be called directly...

SECOND MAID-SERVANT.

They will not send for us... They no longer know what they are doing...

THIRD MAID-SERVANT.

Let us stay here...

FOURTH MAID-SERVANT.

We shall find out somehow when we must go up...

FIFTH MAID—SERVANT.

When the time comes, we shall go without being called...

SIXTH MAID—SERVANT.

There is no sound to be heard in the house...

SEVENTH MAID—SERVANT.

The noise the children are making outside the windows ought to be stopped.

EIGHTH MAID—SERVANT.

They will be quiet presently of themselves.

NINTH MAID—SERVANT.

It is not time yet...

    (*An aged serving-woman enters.*)

THE AGED SERVING—WOMAN.

No one is allowed to go into the room now. I have been listening by the door more than an hour... You could have heard a pin drop... There was no sound...

FIRST MAID—SERVANT.

Have they left her alone in her room?

THE AGED SERVING—WOMAN.

No, no. I think the room is full of people.

FIRST MAID—SERVANT.

They will come, they will come soon...

THE AGED SERVING—WOMAN.

My God! my God, 'tis no good fortune that has come into this house!... It is wrong to speak, but if I could tell what I know...

SECOND MAID—SERVANT.

Was it you who found them at the door?

THE AGED SERVING—WOMAN.

Yes, yes, it was; I found them. The porter says he saw them first, but I woke him up. He was sleeping soundly and it was hard to rouse him. — And now he says he discovered them. Is that fair? — See, I burned myself here in lighting a lamp to go down into the cellar. — Why was I going to the cellar?... I am sure I cannot remember why I was going to the cellar. — Any way, I got up very early, it was not yet very light; I said to myself, I will cross the courtyard and then I will open the door. Well; I went down the staircase on tiptoe and I opened the door just as if it were an ordinary door !... Oh, what a sight I saw! Oh, my God! Imagine what a sight I saw !...

FIRST MAID—SERVANT.
Were they there before the door?

THE AGED SERVING—WOMAN.
They were both lying there before the door!... Like two beggars starved to death... They were close together like two frightened children... The little princess was almost dead, and the sword was still thrust in tall Golaud's side... There was blood upon the sill...

SECOND MAID—SERVANT.
The children must be hushed... They are shouting terribly at the window...

THIRD MAID—SERVANT.
One cannot hear one's self speak...

FOURTH MAID—SERVANT.
There is nothing to be done. I tried to stop them; they will not be still...

FIRST MAID–SERVANT.
I hear that he is almost well.

THE AGED SERVING–WOMAN.
Who ?

FIRST MAID–SERVANT.
The tall Golaud.

THIRD MAID–SERVANT.
Yes, yes ; he was taken a little while ago to his wife's room. I met them in the corridor. He had to be held up like a drunken man. He could not walk alone.

THE AGED SERVING–WOMAN.
He could not kill himself. He is too big and strong. But her wound was a mere nothing, and yet she is dying ?... How can it be ?

FIRST MAID–SERVANT.
Did you see the wound ?

THE AGED SERVING–WOMAN.
As plain as I see you now, daughter. — I saw everything, I tell you... I saw her before anybody did. A tiny wound under her little breast, a tiny wound that would not kill a pigeon. Is that natural ?

FIRST MAID–SERVANT.

Yes, yes; there is some mystery about it...

SECOND MAID–SERVANT.

And it is now three days since her babe was born...

THE AGED SERVING–WOMAN.

Yes, indeed... A babe born on a death-bed! Is not that a great omen? — And such a babe! Have you seen it? — A puny girl, such as a beggar might be ashamed to own... A little waxen thing that came before its time, a little waxen thing only kept alive by being wrapped in wool... No! no! 'tis no good fortune that has come into this house!...

FIRST MAID–SERVANT.

No, it is the hand of God that has done this thing...

SECOND MAID–SERVANT.

It is so indeed; there is justice in all this!

THIRD MAID–SERVANT.

Where is good Prince Pélléas, where is he?... No one knows...

THE AGED SERVING—WOMAN.

Yes, yes, every one knows... But no one dares to say a word... This can't be told... that can't be told... nothing can be told... The truth must not be whispered... But I know that he was found at the bottom of the Fountain of the Blind... But no one, no one was allowed to see him... That is all, that is all; no one will know the rest until the judgment day...

FIRST MAID—SERVANT.

I shall not dare to sleep here again...

THE AGED SERVING—WOMAN.

Yes, yes ; when once misfortune enters a house, silence is in vain...

THIRD MAID—SERVANT.

Yes, it will find you in spite of all.

THE AGED SERVING—WOMAN.

And we cannot go where we will to go...

FOURTH MAID—SERVANT.

We cannot do what we will to do...

FIRST MAID—SERVANT.

They are afraid of us now...

SECOND MAID—SERVANT.
They all keep silence...

THIRD MAID—SERVANT.
They look away when we meet them in
the corridors.

FOURTH MAID—SERVANT.
They only speak in whispers now.

FIFTH MAID—SERVANT.
They behave as if they were all guilty.

SIXTH MAID—SERVANT.
No one knows what they have done.

SEVENTH MAID—SERVANT.
When the masters tremble, what can
we do ?

(*Silence.*)

FIRST MAID—SERVANT.
I no longer hear the children shouting.

SECOND MAID—SERVANT.
They are sitting quietly by the grating.

THIRD MAID—SERVANT.
They are all huddled together.

THE AGED SERVING—WOMAN.
The house is still as death.

FIRST MAID–SERVANT.

Listen, one cannot even hear the chil·
dren breathe...

THE AGED SERVING–WOMAN.

Let us go.   It must be time to go up.

(All go out silently.)

SCENE II.

A ROOM IN THE CASTLE.

*(Arkël, Golaud, and the physician are on
one side of the chamber. Mélisande is in
bed.)*

THE PHYSICIAN.

This trifling wound is not enough to
cause her death, it would not kill a bird...
You are not guilty of her death, prince ;
do not reproach yourself thus...   She
could not have lived. She was born by
chance — to die, and she dies by chance...
And then there still is hope : it may be
we shall save her yet...

ARKËL.

No, no.   Why should we keep such a

silence about her ?... It is ominous !... See how strangely she sleeps — how slow, how slow her breath comes, as though her heart were forever chilled.

GOLAUD.

I killed her for no cause ! I killed her for no cause !... A murder for which the stones might cry out !... They were kissing each other like innocent children !... It was only a kiss... They were brother and sister. And I in a moment — I did it in spite of myself, don't you see !... I did it in spite of myself...

THE PHYSICIAN.

Be silent. She seems to be waking...

MÉLISANDE.

Open the window... Open the window !...

ARKËL.

Shall I open this, Mélisande ?

MÉLISANDE.

No, no, the large window, the large window... I must see !...

ARKËL.

Will not the night air from the sea be
too cold ?

THE PHYSICIAN.

Do as she tells you. Do as she tells
you !

MÉLISANDE.

Thank you...   Is the sun setting ?

ARKËL.

Yes, the sun is setting in the sea.   It
is late.— How are you, Mélisande ?

MÉLISANDE.

Well, well ! — Why do you ask me such
a question ?   I never felt better.— Yet I
know something...

ARKËL.

What do you mean ? —I do not understand...

MÉLISANDE.

I do not understand either quite what I
am saying...   I do not know what I am saying — I do not know what I know...   I no
longer say what I wish...

ARKËL.

No matter, no matter...   I am glad to

hear you speak at all. You have been wandering a little these last few days, and we have not been able to understand a word you said. But that is all over now...

MÉLISANDE.

I do not know... Are you alone here grandfather?

ARKËL.

No, here is the doctor who has cured you!

MÉLISANDE.

Ah!...

ARKËL.

And there is some one else...

MÉLISANDE.

Who?

ARKËL.

It is — do not be frightened!... You may be sure he would not do you the slightest harm. If you are afraid he will go... He is very unhappy...

MÉLISANDE.

Who is it?

ARKËL.

It is... It is your husband... it is
Golaud...

MÉLISANDE.

Is Golaud here ? Why does he not
come to me ?

GOLAUD (*staggering to the bed*).
Mélisande... Mélisande !...

MÉLISANDE.

Is it you, Golaud ? I hardly knew
you... You see the sun is in my eyes...
Why do you look at the wall ?... You are
grown thinner, and you look older... How
long is it since I saw you ?

GOLAUD (*to Arkël and the physician*).

Please, please, go a moment, just a
moment... I will leave the door wide
open... only an instant... I want to say
something to her, something I could not
die without saying... Will you ?... Just
to the end of the corridor. You shall
come back in an instant... Do not refuse
the request of a wretched man. (*Arkël
and the physician go out.*) Mélisande, do
you pity me as I pity you ?... Méli-

sande ?... Can you forgive me, Mélisande ?...

MÉLISANDE.

Yes, yes. I forgive you... What is there
to forgive ?

GOLAUD.

I have wronged you so, Mélisande... I
cannot tell you what evil I have done you ;
yet I feel it now, I feel what it has been
from the first day... I see it all at once
like a flash of lightning... Everything is
my fault, everything that has happened or
is to happen... If I could find words, you
would see it all too as I do... I see it all,
I see it all !... But I loved you so !... I
loved you so ! But now some one is about
to die ! It is I who will soon be no
more !... I should like... I should like to
ask you — you will not be angry with me ?
And the truth must be spoken to one about
to die. I should not rest if I did not
know the truth... Do you swear to tell
me the truth ?

MÉLISANDE.

Yes.

GOLAUD.

Did you love Pélléas ?

MÉLISANDE.

Yes, of course I loved him. — Where is
he ?

GOLAUD.

Do you not understand me ? — Will you
not understand me ? — It seems to me... it
seems to me...   Well, then, it is this : — I
ask you if you loved him with a guilty
love — if you... if you both were guilty ?
Speak, tell me, yes, yes, yes ?...

MÉLISANDE.

No, no ; we were not guilty ! — Why do
you ask me that?

GOLAUD.

Mélisande !...   For the love of God, tell
me the truth !

MÉLISANDE.

Why ?   Have I not told the truth ?

GOLAUD.

Do not perjure yourself — at the point
of death !

MÉLISANDE.

Death ? who is going to die ? — am I ?

GOLAUD.

Yes, you, and I, I too shall follow you !...
There must be truth between us... There
must be truth between us at last, do you
hear ?... Tell me all, tell me all. I will
pardon all !...

MÉLISANDE.

Why am I to die ? — I did not know...

GOLAUD.

You know it now... It is not too late !
It is not too late !... Quick ! quick... The
truth ! the truth !...

MÉLISANDE.

The truth... the truth —

GOLAUD.

Where are you ? — Mélisande ! — Where
are you ? This is strange ! Mélisande,
where are you ? — Where have you gone ?
(*Seeing Arkel and the physician at the
door.*) Yes, yes, you may come in, come
in... I have learned nothing. It was all
in vain... It is too late. She is already

far away from us !... I shall never know...
I shall die here like a blind man !...

ARKËL.

What have you been doing ? You will
kill her...

GOLAUD.

I have killed her...

ARKËL.

Mélisande !...

MÉLISANDE.

Is it you, grandfather ?

ARKËL.

Yes, my child... What can I do for you ?

MÉLISANDE.

Is winter coming already ?

ARKËL.

Why do you ask that ?

MÉLISANDE.

Because it is cold, and I do not see the
leaves...

ARKËL.

Are you cold ? — shall I shut the windows ?

MÉLISANDE.

No, no, not till the sun is beneath the sea. — It sinks so slowly, is not winter near ?

ARKËL.

Yes ! — Do you dislike the winter ?

MÉLISANDE.

Oh, yes, I dread the cold, I dread the bitter cold !...

ARKËL.

Do you feel any easier ?

MÉLISANDE.

Oh, yes, I have no more pain...

ARKËL.

Would you like to see your child ?

MÉLISANDE.

What child ?

ARKËL.

Your child. — You are a mother... You have brought a little daughter into the world...

MÉLISANDE.

Where is she ?

ARKEL.

Here !...

MÉLISANDE.

How strange !... I cannot raise my arms
to take her !...

ARKËL.

You are still so weak...   I will hold her.
Look !...

MÉLISANDE.

She does not smile...   How small she is !
She is crying...   Oh, how I pity her !

(*One after another, the maid-servants
of the castle enter and silently stand about
the walls in expectation.*)

GOLAUD (*starting up*).

What is the meaning of this ? — Why
have all these women come ?...

PHYSICIAN.

They are the serving-women.

ARKËL.

Who gave them permission to come ?

PHYSICIAN.

It was not I...

GOLAUD.

Why have you come here? — No one gave you permission... What did you come for? — What is it? — Speak!...

(*The servants are silent.*)

ARKËL.

Do not speak so loud... She is falling asleep. Her eyes are closed...

GOLAUD.

It is not...?

PHYSICIAN.

No, no; see, she breathes!

ARKËL.

Her eyes are full of tears. — Her spirit is weeping... Why does she try to stretch out her arms? — What does she wish?

PHYSICIAN.

It is to embrace her child! Mother's love is struggling against...

GOLAUD.

Is it coming? — Speak! I must know — speak!...

PHYSICIAN.

It may be.

GOLAUD.

Already?... My God, I must make her hear me...— Mélisande, Mélisande !... Leave us alone together, leave me alone with her !...

ARKËL.

No, do not come near her now... Do not disturb her... Do not speak to her. You know not the mysteries of the spirit...

GOLAUD.

It is not my doing... It is not my doing !...

ARKËL.

Do you hear me? She must not be troubled. Speak lower now...— The human soul is silent, it must tread its path by itself... It passes and suffers and shrinks alone... The pity of it, Golaud, — ah, the pity of it !

(*At this moment all the servants suddenly kneel in the background.*)

ARKËL (*turning round*).
What was that ?

PHYSICIAN (*approaching the bed and examining the body*).
They are right !　　　　(*Long silence.*)

ARKËL.

I saw no change. — Are you sure?

PHYSICIAN.

Yes, yes.

ARKËL.

I heard nothing... So suddenly, so swiftly... And she has gone without speaking!

GOLAUD (*sobbing*).

Oh! Oh! Oh!

ARKËL.

Come, Golaud... The dead must rest in peace... Come, come !... It is terrible, but it was not your doing... She was a poor, helpless little one, a mystery, as every human being is... See how she lies there as though she was only her infant's elder sister... Come, come !... My God! My God !... It is all beyond my comprehension !... Let us not remain here. — Come; the child must not stay in this chamber of death... It must live and take her place — poor little babe !

(*They go out in silence.*)